Cross & Shield Ministries
Senior Chaplain Paul Northcut
chaplain.northcut@gmail.com
479-264-6146 P O Box 44
Russellville, AR 72811

Beyond Belief

There Is More to God Than We Perceive

Patrick D. McElroy

Beyond Belief
by Patrick D. McElroy
Copyright ©2007 Patrick D. McElroy

All rights reserved. This book is protected under the copyright laws of the United States of America. This book may not be copied or reprinted for commercial gain or profit. Unless otherwise identified, Scripture quotations are from the King James Version of the Bible.

ISBN 1-58169-235-8
For Worldwide Distribution
Printed in the U.S.A.

Axiom Press
P.O. Box 191540 • Mobile, AL 36619
800-367-8203

Table of Contents

Acknowledgments

I thank my parents, Eddie and Della, for bringing me into this world and not stopping with that accomplishment. I thank my sisters, Delores, Angela, Yolanda, and niece Daina for supporting me in all my endeavors. Thank you, prayer partners Chuvalo and "Mac," for holding a brother before the Lord.

In terms of this specific book, I thank my early reviewers, Sylvia and Sherry, for critical feedback, and their husbands, Terry and Jonnie, for encouraging me prior to the first draft when we co-taught a Bible study together. Thank you, Dan and Pastor Walter Kimbrough, for giving comments on a later draft. Thank you, Sister Perri, for being an instrument in my transformation.

I especially want to thank every Bible study student who challenged me to be prepared for class and helped me refine the concepts in this book during class discussions.

Most of all, I want to thank the Lord God Almighty for persistently and patiently waiting on me to seek Him first.

Preface

Suppose you have a really great friend; you would probably introduce her or him to your other friends over time. After all, good people need to meet other good people, right? Similarly, I have such a friend but it was not always this way. I met him when I was a child. We had one of those friendships that ebbed and flowed, like most relationships. It wasn't until some 20 years later that I discovered something that troubled me.

I knew people who were friends with my friend, but their relationship was different. They were much closer to my friend than I. As a result of this closeness, these individuals were doing better in all dimensions of their lives. They were benefiting more than me by knowing my friend better than I knew him. Somehow, they discovered that there was more to this friendship than I initially perceived.

The really bothersome issue is that my friend was not petty and did not play favorites. Everyone could have the same benefits. I knew that much about his character. Thus, I resolved to change the nature of our relationship. I committed to get to know my friend in every possible way.

Reading this book will introduce (or reintroduce) you to my Friend, the Lord Jesus Christ. Overwhelmingly, most U.S. citizens express belief in God. The power to live the more abundant life that Christ promises is much deeper than a cursory acknowledgement of God's existence.

This is not a book on religion. This is a book about the most important relationship in which we can ever participate. I had a solid belief in God for a long time. The relationship was real, but not nearly as intimate as was possible. This book is about going beyond a belief to living the exceptional life that is available to every person. When one experiences the intimate fellowship available in Christ, it is unimaginable to go back to a business-as-usual belief system.

This book begins with a refresher on the foundation needed before entering into a relationship with Jesus Christ. While it may not be necessary for every reader, the review can serve as preparation for a conversation with someone who "does not get it," yet. Likewise, a person who did not grow up in the church will not find this book intimidating. The chapters are short but packed with revelation. Each chapter builds upon the previous chapter and the book concludes with a challenge for every reader.

Chapter 1

The Dilemma

Paul, the apostle and founder of many churches in early Christianity, summarized the human condition this way:

I don't understand myself at all, for I really want to do what is right, but I don't do it. Instead, I do the very thing I hate. I know perfectly well that what I am doing is wrong, and my bad conscience shows that I agree that the law is good. But I can't help myself, because it is sin inside me that makes me do these evil things. I know I am rotten through and through so far as my old sinful nature is concerned. No matter which way I turn, I can't make myself do right. I want to, but I can't. When I want to do good, I don't. And when I try not to do wrong, I do it anyway. But if I am doing what I don't want to do, I am not really the one doing it; the sin within me is doing it.

It seems to be a fact of life that when I want to do what is right, I inevitably do what is wrong. I love God's law with all my heart. But there is another law at work within me that is at war with my mind. This law wins the fight and makes me a slave to the sin that is still within me. Oh, what a miserable person I am! Who will free me from this life that is dominated by sin? Thank God! The answer is in Jesus Christ our Lord. So you see how it is: In my mind I really want to obey God's law, but because of my sinful nature I am a slave to sin (Romans 7:15-25 NLT).

Human beings inherited the result of Adam and Eve's decision to disobey God in the Garden of Eden. *Therefore, just as sin entered the world through one man, and death through sin, and in this way death came to all men, because all sinned….* Referred to as our sinful nature, these tendencies are parts of our spiritual genetic code. Much like two-year-olds insisting on having their own way (even to their detriment), we drift away from God to become our own god. The remedy is to consistently seek God through holy living.

We cannot think of our personal behavior in terms of good and bad because most of us do not consider ourselves as wicked; *…no one is good but One, that is, God.* Subsequently, we grade ourselves on a scale of behavior. In the spiritual realm, there is no scale, only two absolute possibilities: God versus evil. We have a spiritual choice to make: either follow God's plan or follow our natural tendencies.

God is still in control of the world; even so, we often forfeit our authority in this realm to Satan when we disobey God (just like Adam did). Nevertheless, there is hope in Jesus Christ, for God provided Jesus as our way back to Him. When we become followers of Jesus Christ, the Holy Spirit empowers us to conquer the sinful nature that resides within each of us.

Temptation

No temptation has overtaken you except such as is common to man; but God is faithful, who will not allow you to be tempted beyond what you are able … Temptation is part of the human experience. *Jesus was led by the Spirit into the desert to be tempted by the devil.* If Jesus was tempted, why would we think that we will not be tempted? Perhaps we should shift our perspective on temptation. Consider that temptation is an opportunity to prove our loyalty to God. Without the temptation, how could we really prove our allegiance?

Temptation continues to assail us. Yet, it is reassuring to know that temptation is not new or unique to any human being. The blessing is that there is *always* a way out of the temptation. The Bible promises that the escape from temptation is always divinely presented. Our challenge is to abandon our affinity for that specific sin and desperately search for an escape even in the midst of the temptation. This is where willpower, faith in Jesus, and the power of the Holy Spirit combine for spiritual victory.

Willpower is effective only to the degree that we *submit to God and resist the devil*. When we start to view the sin as ugly and revolting as God sees it, then we are on the path to victory. Through willpower, we submit our predicament to Jesus knowing that without Him, we are defeated (again). By faith, we hang on as best we can, trusting that the Holy Spirit will provide the escape from the temptation that we are experiencing. The manifestation of the escape is personal, and will cost us our pride—at the very least—as we humble ourselves before God, asking Him to deliver us while depending upon His response.

Regardless of how we escape and no matter how many bruises we acquire during our escape, we live to battle another day. It is, however, not wise to continue in this crisis mode of operation or we will be defeated eventually and even worse, we mock God. As we mature spiritually, our key to victory is avoiding the first stages of the temptation by *the renewing of our mind*. The Holy Spirit and the Bible will counsel us on how to avoid this particular temptation in the future. Understand that in this life, we will never be completely free of temptations, but we can learn to recognize them better and avoid many situations altogether.

The Bible specifically mentions that Christians are not to love the world, be friends with the world, or get "caught up" in the world system. Built upon the principles of greed, power, status, and lust (to name just a few), the world system encourages a self-centered, compromising, "anything goes" lifestyle that directly contrasts with God's standard for living.

One of the seemingly innocent principles of the world system is self-interest or self-determination, which Satan often perverts into selfish ambition. Such self-centeredness or promotion of oneself to a god status leads to idolatry and pride. Pride is the very reason why God kicked Satan out of heaven! Even our own minds can deceive us. Often, we criticize Adam and Eve for their foolishness in messing up a good thing in the Garden of Eden; yet we rebel against God in our simple, everyday decisions.

Romans 5:12 – Therefore, just as sin entered the world through one man, and death through sin, and in this way death came to all men, because all sinned. (NIV)

Mark 10:18 – So Jesus said to him, "Why do you call Me good? No one is good but One, that is, God." (NIV)

1 Cor. 10:13 – No temptation has overtaken you except such as is common to man; but God is faithful, who will not allow you to be tempted beyond what you are able, but with the temptation will also make the way of escape, that you may be able to bear it. (NKJV)

Romans 12:2 – Do not conform any longer to the pattern of this world, but be transformed by the renewing of your mind. Then you will be able to test and approve what God's will is—his good, pleasing and perfect will. (NIV)

Chapter 2

The Standard

Freedom does not mean the absence of constraints or moral absolutes. Suppose a skydiver at 10,000 feet announces to the rest of the group, "I'm not using a parachute this time. I want freedom!"

The fact is that a skydiver is constrained by a greater law—the law of gravity. But when the skydiver chooses the "constraint" of the parachute, she is free to enjoy the exhilaration. God's moral laws act the same way: They restrain, but they are absolutely necessary to enjoy the exhilaration of real freedom.[1]

In the Old Testament, Moses received the Law of God after the Israelites left Egypt so that they would know how God wanted them to conduct themselves. The Ten Commandments is the most famous portion of the Law; however, there are many more rules and regulations that are mostly documented in the book of Leviticus. The penalties for breaking the Law were very punitive. In extreme, but not rare cases, the person was put to death for breaking God's law. Other cases required a purification ritual. Often, God accepted an animal sacrifice in place of the person as the penalty for the sin.

Established to demonstrate how God desires for us to live, the Law also shows us how far we have strayed from God's original intent. It works in a similar manner as guidelines that parents establish for their children. For example, parents set curfews or restrictions for their teenagers not as a form of punishment, but as a means of protection from potentially dangerous situations. Teenagers will not become truly aware of this benefit until much later in life, especially if they have children. God's Law works the same way for us. Like teenagers; however, we rebel against the constraints out of ignorance of the larger perspective and focus on our own narrow agenda. Much like teenagers, we often create unnecessary drama in our lives by writing our own rules.

Fulfilling the Law

Jesus clarified that His purpose on earth was not to eliminate the Law that Moses documented, *Do not think that I have come to abolish the Law or the Prophets; I have not come to abolish them but to fulfill them*. Instead, Jesus' purpose was to give us the power to fulfill and exceed those laws. The Holy Spirit empowers us to mature in Christ and to surpass God's minimum requirements as recorded in the Law. Following God's rules by itself does not guarantee eternal life with God; nonetheless, our behavior should reflect our profession of faith. Because we believe in and love God, we have the motivation to follow His prescription for living.

God requires holy living or "righteousness," which simply means, "right standing" with God or obedience to His directives. As humans, we often compare ourselves to each other. Most of us compare favorably against the latest national serial killer or even the local sexual predator. Such an approach ensures that there is always someone a little better than or a little worse than us. Interestingly, children also use this approach to life until lovingly corrected by their parents. This philosophy permits us to move along the continuum of human behavior while holding on to the concept that everyone is going to heaven except the really bad people.

So how bad is bad? How many "evil points" are required before we are condemned to hell? Can a murderer ever go to heaven given this approach to morality? The good news is that even the worst of the worst can be redeemed through Jesus; however, there is a price.

Holiness

God has one standard: holiness. *Be holy, because I am holy.* Not "long church robes," "degrees from theology school," or full time ministry types of holiness, but a practical obedience to God's directions. This expectation eliminates sliding scale morality or situational ethics, which has become a convenient justification for our sinful behavior. Because none of us can achieve holiness without Him, God the Father gave us Jesus so that through Him the penalty for our sinfulness has been paid. Once we have accepted the redemption of Jesus, we become different in our spirit and become capable of living up to God's requirement that we behave differently. We do not have to clean ourselves up before we go to God. In fact, we could not do it even if we tried. If we could rectify all of our problems before coming to God, there would be no need for God! We should allow God to cleanse us thoroughly, which He has promised to do. He is the only one qualified to do the job.

It is possible to confuse righteousness with self-righteousness. By definition, self-righteousness refers to right standing according to our personal moral code—not God's. How do we know when we are treading in self-righteousness? When we begin a sentence with phrases like, "at least I am not like..." or "at least I do not...," we often place ourselves above someone we deem a little less holy than us. Our gold standard is Jesus Christ, whose holiness we cannot surpass. The crucial question is, "where is the holiness in our (not our neighbor's) character?" We are only responsible for our own beliefs and actions even though it is so easy to see the shortcomings of another person.

Benefits

The beauty of holy living is that believers not only get the eternal reward, but also receive tangible and intangible benefits while on earth. Two tangible benefits of holy living are sexual health (from avoiding sexual impurity that may lead to sexually transmitted diseases) and civil liberty (from avoiding dishonest practices that can land one in jail). Some intangible benefits of holy living include the following: *love, joy, peace, patience, kindness, gentleness, and self-control*. As hard as it may try, the world cannot duplicate the benefits of holy living. Imagine that people all over the world spend hundreds of millions of dollars annually on drugs, medications, and alcohol in a futile attempt to achieve peace—the peace which *transcends all understanding*. This peace only comes from God and there are no harmful side effects!

God does not promise us a "bed of roses" or a lifetime of leisure for believing in Him. He tells us in His Word that we will experience suffering and confront challenges even though we follow Him. God also promises us that He will take care of His believers and the pain is worth the reward. The critical issue is belonging to God.

One of the benefits of belonging is receiving the rules of the game. It would be dangerous for us to play football in a baseball uniform simply because we prefer it that way. Likewise, living life according to rules we made up could be an exercise in futility. God's rules are for our protection and ultimately our success in eternity. Thus, the dilemma described at the start of the previous chapter can be effectively resolved for every individual. Resolving the dilemma does not instantly make life an easy journey, but it does determine our eternal destination. Additionally, it answers the nagging question, "Is there more to life than this?" I learned there is much more to God than we might imagine. The miracle is that while He can't reveal everything about Himself to us, He is willing to show us more than we think we know.

Just as the law of gravity as depicted in the start of this chapter cannot be successfully ignored for a long period of time, God's constraints will prevail. These constraints are ultimately for our good, even though we may not perceive them that way.

> *Matthew 5:17 – Think not that I am come to destroy the law, or the prophets: I am not come to destroy, but to fulfill.*

> *1 Peter 1:14-16 – As obedient children, do not conform to the evil desires you had when you lived in ignorance. But just as he who called you is holy, so be holy in all you do; for it is written: "Be holy, because I am holy."*

> *Phil. 4:6-7 – Do not be anxious about anything, but in everything, by prayer and petition, with thanksgiving, present your requests to God. And the peace of God, which transcends all understanding, will guard your hearts and your minds in Christ Jesus. (NIV)*

> *Psalm 34:19 – Many are the afflictions of the righteous: but the LORD delivereth him out of them all.*

[1] Edward K.Rowell, *1001 Quotes, Illustrations & Humorous Stories* for preachers, teachers and writers. (Grand Rapids, MI: Baker Books, 2005), p.268.

Chapter 3

The User's Manual

A TV news camera crew was on assignment in southern Florida filming the widespread destruction of Hurricane Andrew. In one scene, amid the devastation and debris stood one house on its foundation. The owner was cleaning up the yard when a reporter approached him.

"Sir, why is your house the only one still standing?" asked the reporter. "How did you manage to escape the severe damage of the hurricane?" "I built this house myself," the man replied. "I also built it according to the Florida state building code. When the code called for two-by-six trusses, I used two-by-six trusses. I was told that a house built according to code could withstand a hurricane. I did, and it did. I suppose no one else around here followed the code."

When the sun is shining and the skies are blue, building our lives on something other than the guidelines in God's Word can be tempting. But there's only one way to be ready for a storm.[1]

The Bible is the Word of God and contains all we need to know about God. It does not contain all there is to know about God; no book or volume of books could handle such a task. Sometimes, the Bible is challenged because of its incompleteness from a historical perspective. However, the challengers fail to realize that it was not intended to be a complete historical record. The Bible is also challenged because men authored it. On the contrary, the Bible says that it was "inspired" by God, so He authored it by giving men the words to document.

Unlike a novel, the Bible is living and breathing. The Holy Spirit reveals what the Bible is saying, which explains why non-believers just "don't get it." In contrast, Christians can unlock Biblical truths by faith through revelation from the Holy Spirit. This is the secret to unveiling the mysteries of the Bible. If we do not avail ourselves to the Holy Spirit, then we refuse access to the only "interpreter" capable to translate the Bible for us. This is comparable to us going to a foreign land where we have a friend who is bilingual, yet we refuse to call her. We stubbornly attempt to make do with clumsy body language and a cheap translation book. Sadly, the trip is not as beneficial as it could have been because we wasted a precious resource by rejecting a willing translator.

The paradox between God's thinking and human thinking as recorded in the Bible does not make sense in human terms. *Bless those who persecute you; bless and do not curse*. That sounds crazy, yet the Bible says, *For the wisdom of this world is foolishness with God....* The Bible is not designed to make sense in terms of human knowledge; it is a spiritual document and reading it is a spiritual experience.

Furthermore, the Bible is challenged because of its age, yet we celebrate the longevity of human institutions with words such as "since 1905" or "established 1850." God in His infinite wisdom makes His Word available to us. *All Scripture is God-breathed and is useful for teaching, rebuking, correcting and training in righteousness....* Since human frailties such as unforgiveness, disobedience, and sexual immorality noted in the Bible still exist today, the Word of God continues to have relevance for our lives. Not only does the Word of God precede us, it will last forever. *Heaven and earth shall pass away: but my words shall not pass away.*

It is impossible to achieve success in life without learning and applying eternal truth to our lives. We begin our interaction with the truth via divine revelation of who God is by God Himself, since we do not discover God on our own. God then reveals to us the truth of who we are in Him. He makes this everlasting truth available to us through His word. We either believe that the Bible is God's word or we do not.

There are over six billion people on earth; yet there cannot be six billion truths. In fact, human error in perception ensures that people will have different interpretations of the truth. This is why courts of law rely on the testimony of many witnesses to establish the truth.

Truth does not change over time. Think about statements that were once regarded as "truth" by former generations. One such "truth" insisted that the world was flat. People also once believed that the sun revolved around the earth. Obviously these statements are not true, and were never true despite their popularity within the scientific community of the day. Even today, what scientists present as "fact" is basically an agreed upon theory by very smart people awaiting more evidence over time.

In the spiritual realm, we cannot discover the truth; God has to reveal it to us. Our human perspective is too narrow and our lives are too short to discover the truth. Basically, our opinions are irrelevant to the existence of the truth. God reveals Himself to us through our faith in Him. *Jesus saith unto him, I am the way, the truth, and the life….* Truth is dependent upon proper perspective and only God Almighty has the best perspective to see the truth. We can deny there is a truth, and we can deny the truth when God reveals it to us; however, we experience dire consequences if we choose either of these options.

Understanding everything in the Bible is not a condition for believing it all as truth. We do not understand how most of the devices in this world operate, yet we trust that they will perform as designed by people we will never meet. For example, we propel ourselves around town in vehicles weighing several tons with only a thin, double-yellow paint strip separating us from oncoming traffic. In spite of that, we trust that every driver will adhere to the rules of driving. In the event of an accident we trust the airbag and seatbelt to save us. If only we had that type of faith in God!

Unlocking the Secrets

The Bible tells us all we need to know about God and ourselves. It also gives us the instructions or building code on how to live as God intends for us. Moreover, the Bible unlocks the secret to success; *meditate on it day and night, so that you may be careful to do everything written in it. Then you will be prosperous and successful*. Finally, the Bible is the truth revealed by God *...and the truth shall make you free*. Personal application of the truth increases the intimate fellowship to which God invites each of us.

Young children of veterans killed in action are sometimes blessed to receive letters from that particular parent upon reaching the maturity to handle such material. These letters provide a glimpse of who the parent was in their own words. The parents may also dole out advice they knew they would not be available to dispense later. Most of all, the writings reflect the love that the parent had for the child, a love that the parent wanted to immortalize through documentation. Word-of-mouth stories from those who knew the parent are good, but the letters and notes are priceless. God has inspired the writing of a series of letters and notes to humankind. Peppered with instruction and guidance, the love theme oozes from every passage, even those where disciplinary action is applied. Very few adults would ignore the letters from a deceased parent that they never really got to know. God's letters are much more empowering and beneficial to us and He is lovingly extending us the invitation to read them.

As I began to read the Bible as an adult away from the mandate of a parent or teacher, I started to change. Slowly I began to abandon my childlike perception on the stories in the Bible to apply adult maturity to the depicted situations. No longer were the stories cute, but troubling in that I sometimes struggled with the same issues as the main characters. My thirst for the word grew and simply reading alone was not enough. I began attending group Bible study as an adult for the first time. This allowed for correction when I was misinterpreting the lessons, something that could not occur in a group of one. Unknowingly, I had begun a journey to a place that I was unaware of at the time.

Romans 12:14 – Bless them which persecute you: bless, and curse not.

1 Cor. 3:19 – For the wisdom of this world is foolishness with God. For it is written, He taketh the wise in their own craftiness.

2 Tim. 3:16-17 – All Scripture is God-breathed and is useful for teaching, rebuking, correcting and training in righteousness, so that the man of God may be thoroughly equipped for every good work. (NIV)

Luke 21:33 – Heaven and earth shall pass away: but my words shall not pass away.

John 1:1 – In the beginning was the Word, and the Word was with God, and the Word was God. He was in the beginning with God. (NKJV)

John 14:6 – Jesus saith unto him, I am the way, the truth, and the life: no man cometh unto the Father, but by me.

John 8:31-32 – Then Jesus said to those Jews who believed Him, "If you abide in My word, you are My disciples indeed. And you shall know the truth, and the truth shall make you free." (NKJV)

1 Cor. 2:12-14 – We have not received the spirit of the world but the Spirit who is from God, that we may understand what God has freely given us. This is what we speak, not in words taught us by human wisdom but in words taught by the Spirit, expressing spiritual truths in spiritual words. The man without the Spirit does not accept the things that come from the Spirit of God, for they are foolishness to him, and he cannot understand them, because they are spiritually discerned. (NIV)

Joshua 1:8 – Do not let this Book of the Law depart from your mouth; meditate on it day and night, so that you may be careful to do everything written in it. Then you will be prosperous and successful. (NIV)

[1] Edward K.Rowell, *1001 Quotes, Illustrations & Humorous Stories* for preachers, teachers and writers. (Grand Rapids MI: Baker Books, 2005), p.331.

Chapter 4

The Misunderstanding

"Eating lunch at a small café, Mark Reed of Camarillo, California, saw a sparrow hop through the open door and peck at the crumbs near his table. When the crumbs were gone, the sparrow hopped to the window ledge, spread its wings, and took flight. Brief flight. It crashed against the windowpane and fell to the floor.

The bird quickly recovered and tried again. Crash. And again. Crash.

Mark got up and attempted to shoo the sparrow out the door, but the closer he got, the harder it threw itself against the pane. He nudged it with his hand. That sent the sparrow fluttering along the ledge, hammering its beak at the glass.

Finally, Mark reached out and gently caught the bird, folding his fingers around its wings and body. It weighted almost nothing. He thought of how powerless and vulnerable the sparrow must have felt. At the door he released it, and the sparrow sailed away.

As Mark did with the sparrow, God takes us captive only to set us free."[1]

Perhaps our perspective on God is too small. ...*What is man that you are mindful of him, the son of man that you care for him?* We really don't understand God. *For my thoughts are not your thoughts, neither are your ways my ways, saith the LORD*. God is real, living, conscious, and concerned about each of us. He is not a theory, a concept, nor a mere "higher consciousness." Human beings are obviously conscious, so how can the unconscious birth or create the conscious? In Genesis, we learn of God's creation of the earth, the sky, the heavenly realm, people, animals, and plants. It is an insult to attempt to reduce God to a detached, uncaring inanimate object. It is also disrespectful to dismiss God's initiation of creation just because we have disassociated ourselves from Him and cannot fully understand Him.

Atheists believe there is no God or any other supernatural entities. Agnostics believe there is not enough proof to affirm or deny the existence of God—there might be a God, but no one knows for sure because there is not enough so-called evidence. The reason why arguments such as these are invalid is because God says, *But without faith it is impossible to please him: for he that cometh to God must believe that he is, and that he is a rewarder of them that diligently seek him*. Thus, God reveals Himself AFTER we demonstrate our belief that He exists.

Atheists and agnostics make very bold statements about the existence of God. They will be rewarded eternally for their beliefs—one way or another. Nevertheless, it would be tragic for a believer or Christian to miss eternal salvation because of serious errors in belief and understanding.

Sovereignty

God is sovereign. Sovereignty is independence from external control over a defined set of borders. Jesus often spoke about the "kingdom" of God. Unlike democratic nations ruled "by the people," kingdoms do not hold elections. There is no higher authority in any kingdom than the king, and the king is not directed by the opinions of his subjects. In the spiritual realm, the kingdom of God works in the same manner. God is the *King of kings and Lord of lords*; He is all-present, all-knowing, and all-powerful. There is none like Him. Because He is the Most Sovereign, God has the authority to do whatever He wants to do, whenever He desires, wherever He chooses. The only limits on God are those that He places upon Himself.

The Trinity

God is represented through the Holy Trinity. The Holy Trinity or Godhead—which includes God the Father, God the Son, and God the Holy Spirit—is difficult for our finite minds to grasp. We often think in the tangible terms of a three-dimensional world, which will not work in the spiritual realm. *God is a spirit*. He made us in His image, thus we also are spirits; spirits with bodies, not bodies with spirits. Yet we persist in our attempts to reduce God to a physical entity because it is what we understand.

Here is an example to help illustrate the Holy Trinity: Think about water, ice, and steam. It is all water, but each has distinguishing differences for specific purposes. Together, God the Father, God the Son, and God the Holy Spirit work the same way. Each is God individually and all are God collectively.

God the Father has done everything possible to enable us to reconcile the spiritual breach from Him initially caused by Adam. The Father sent Jesus, the Son, to demonstrate the way back to Him and pay the penalty for this breach. Jesus sent the Holy Spirit to guide and direct believers after He returned to heaven. God the Father communes with Jesus and the Holy Spirit who both intercede on our behalf according to His agenda. *We do not know what we ought to pray for, but the Spirit Himself intercedes for us with groans that words cannot express*.

As with the bird in the beginning of this chapter, we often do not recognize when God is helping us. We then resist His overtures and create needless turmoil in our lives. As with the man in the story, God is patient and persistent to accomplish His purpose. God has worked out the entire plan for us. *"For I know the plans I have for you," declares the LORD , "plans to prosper you and not to harm you, plans to give you hope and a future.*" All we have to do is sign up for the "program," which is a relationship and then nurture it until it blossoms. The invitation is real and persistent for each of us, but the choice to respond is ours alone.

Psalm 8:3-5 – When I consider your heavens, the work of your fingers, the moon and the stars, which you have set in place, what is man that you are mindful of him, the son of man that you care for him?

Isaiah 55:8-9 – For my thoughts are not your thoughts, neither are your ways my ways, saith the LORD. For as the heavens are higher than the earth, so are my ways higher than your ways, and my thoughts than your thoughts.

Hebrews 11:6 – But without faith it is impossible to please him: for he that cometh to God must believe that he is, and that he is a rewarder of them that diligently seek him.

1 Tim, 6:15-16 – ...God, the blessed and only Ruler, the King of kings and Lord of lords, who alone is immortal and who lives in unapproachable light, whom no one has seen or can see. To him be honor and might forever. Amen.

Psalm 86:8 – Among the gods there is none like you, O Lord; no deeds can compare with yours.

Romans 8:26-27 – In the same way, the Spirit helps us in our weakness. We do not know what we ought to pray for, but the Spirit himself intercedes for us with groans that words cannot express. And he who searches our hearts knows the mind of the Spirit, because the Spirit intercedes for the saints in accordance with God's will. (NIV)

Jer. 29:11-12 – For I know the plans I have for you," declares the LORD, "plans to prosper you and not to harm you, plans to give you hope and a future. Then you will call upon me and come and pray to me, and I will listen to you . (NIV)

Genesis 1:1 – In the beginning God created the heaven and the earth.

John 4:24 – God is a Spirit: and they that worship him must worship him in spirit and in truth.

Eph. 4:4-6 – There is one body, and one Spirit, even as ye are called in one hope of your calling; One Lord, one faith, one baptism, One God and Father of all, who is above all, and through all, and in you all.

Psalms 24:10 – Who is he, this King of glory? The LORD Almighty—he is the King of glory.

[1] Edward K.Rowell , *1001 Quotes,* for preachers, teachers and writers. (Grand Rapids MI: Baker Books, 2005), p.269.

Chapter 5

The Power

> I have a glove here in my hand. The glove cannot do anything by itself, but when my hand is in it, it can do many things. True, it is not the glove, but my hand in the glove that acts. We are gloves. It is the Holy Spirit in us who is the hand, who does the job. We have to make room for the hand so that every finger is filled.[1]

As we have seen in the previous chapter, the Holy Spirit is the third person of the Holy Trinity. *Now the earth was formless and empty, darkness was over the surface of the deep, and the Spirit of God was hovering over the waters*. God the Holy Spirit, often known as the "Spirit of God" in the Old Testament of the Bible, was introduced to us in Genesis as a participant in creation. The Spirit of God also provided for temporary, supernatural strength to King Saul, David, and others to do God the Father's will. In the New Testament following Jesus' baptism, we observe the Spirit descending upon Him like a dove. *Then a voice came from heaven, "You are My beloved Son, in whom I am well pleased."* The Spirit of God also descended upon Jesus to supernaturally empower Him to do God the Father's will during His earthly ministry.

The Holy Spirit is real, living, and active in this world. When Jesus ascended to heaven, He sent the Holy Spirit to be with believers during our life on earth. It is the Holy Spirit who draws us into receiving Jesus Christ as our Lord and Savior. Every believer has access to this same Holy Spirit simultaneously, whereas when He was on the earth, Jesus could only be in one place at one time because He was in human form. The key to experiencing the Holy Spirit is to receive Him by faith, i.e., without evidence, and to submit to His power, authority, agenda and timing; otherwise, we will remain spiritually vulnerable.

The Holy Spirit's Character and Role

The Holy Spirit has character traits that include: *love, joy, peace, patience, kindness, goodness, faithfulness, gentleness, and self-control*. We may not initially possess these qualities, but over time they should manifest themselves within us as believers. Just as an apple tree is an apple tree because it produces apples (and not pears), so should believers produce spiritual fruit that reflects the character of God.

God the Holy Spirit plays a specific role in the life of a believer. As part of the Godhead, His role is to comfort, teach, guide, and empower us to live the life that God the Father requires. Our most powerful ally in this world, the Holy Spirit enables us to conquer our sinful nature and convicts us of our separation from God. Furthermore, the Holy Spirit gives us the supernatural ability to accomplish God's will on earth. The Holy Spirit also prays for us to receive the things that the Father wants us to have. *Likewise the Spirit also helps in our weaknesses. For we do not know what we should pray for as we ought, but the Spirit Himself makes intercession for us with groanings that cannot be uttered.*

Baptism and Filling of the Holy Spirit

Now it is God who has made us for this very purpose and has given us the Spirit as a deposit, guaranteeing what is to come.

Believers receive the "deposit of the Holy Spirit" instantly upon our acceptance of Jesus Christ as our Lord and Savior. So exactly what is this deposit? This deposit or "mark" of God signals that believers belong to God and it occurs when the Holy Spirit takes up residence in our hearts. It works like a spiritual identification mechanism—only better.

"The baptism of the Holy Spirit is intended to clothe us with supernatural power from on high so that we can be witnesses."[2] "With the Holy Spirit baptism, we are all 'baptized into' the oneness of the body. That is the purpose of the baptism in the Spirit."[3] The baptism is a supernatural coming down of the Holy Ghost over the believer, immersing him not in water but in the shekinah glory of God's presence. Whether it is visible or not is not the important question."[4]

This event can be very emotional for some people; however, "when the Bible speaks of the baptism in the Holy Spirit, in no case is there any direct reference to any kind of emotion, whatever."[5] In our clumsy attempts to describe God, we grasp at what we know (emotion), but this can mislead people into believing they do not have something that God already gave them. Additionally, emotion can deceive us into believing that God gave us something that He did not give us. Some people weep uncontrollably when they receive the Holy Spirit. Others react more energetically by running around the room, shaking, shouting or any combination of these responses. This does not mean that if we do not have any of these experiences that our baptism is any less valid.

The filling of the Holy Spirit occurs when the Holy Spirit increases in position from "deposit" of God within us to "manager" according to God's desires over our lives. Whereas the baptism in the Holy Spirit occurs when we receive Jesus Christ, the filling of the Holy Spirit occurs when we surrender control of our lives to

God. It is as if we have a sign on us that says "Under new management." Likewise, the filling of the Holy Spirit can be a very emotional event when we realize it. Nevertheless, we have to be careful to not "box" God into a certain way of action by presupposing that everyone's experience should mirror ours exactly.

The difference between baptism in the Holy Spirit and the filling of the Holy Spirit is that baptism occurs when a believer receives Jesus Christ. That is what makes us a Christian, a believer. The filling occurs when we surrender control of our lives to God. This makes us powerful Christians. For some people both incidents occur at the same moment, for others years may pass before control is yielded and the filling occurs. This was my situation. I did not know about yielding. I assumed and perhaps was even taught (or at least allowed to believe) that agreeing with God about my situation and the water baptism was all I had to do to resolve my dilemma.

Yielding to the Holy Spirit

Upon my yielding to the authority of the Holy Spirit, my life changed forever. A simple analogy is the experience one has upon getting prescription glasses for the first time. The world looks different. The colors are more vivid and life appears more vibrant. Of course the spiritual difference is more impacting, but this is a brief attempt to describe the change in easily understandable terms.

It is arguable that one can perceive themselves to be a Christian and not yield total control of our life to God. We do this by confessing Jesus Christ as Savior, honestly believing Him to be the Son of God raised from the dead, yet neglecting the lordship of Jesus. An example is noted in the bumper sticker, "God is my co-pilot." Think about that motto for a minute. If we use the car as an analogy for our life, this saying places the most qualified person to guide and direct the car in the secondary position. If God is in the car, why not let Him drive? Likewise, if God is in our life, why not let Him be in charge?

We have to yield our will, desire and actions to the Holy Spirit in order to truly benefit from the deposit of the Holy Spirit. Jesus did not impose Himself on any potential disciples and all of us are potential disciples. He issued and continues to issue an invitation. Likewise, the Holy Spirit will not conduct a hostile takeover of our lives. He simply awaits our reply to Jesus' offer of an abundant life now and eternal life with God.

The Holy Spirit additionally provides us with our spiritual gift(s), or the supernatural ability used to edify the Church, upon our acceptance of Jesus Christ as Lord and Savior. Every believer has at least one spiritual gift. While all humans have natural talents, only believers have spiritual gifts. Talents are not spiritual gifts, although they can appear similar in some cases. Again, the purpose of a spiritual gift is to build up the Church, not the individual upon whom the gift was bestowed.

For example, some people have the natural ability to sing and can hit every note correctly. In contrast, the resident "mother" of the church may not know the musical scales and hums the words she cannot remember; nevertheless, there is not a dry eye in the congregation when she finishes a classic hymn. This happens because although the natural singer may perform a song well, the Holy Spirit empowered the "mother" of the church through several spiritual gifts, thereby allowing her imperfect delivery to touch every willing heart in the room.

The Holy Spirit is our best advocate. He speaks to the Father on our behalf and gives us directions from the Father. The layers of spiritual middle management have been removed and the communication cannot be any more pure. We have observed in business how this technique allows a company to become more effective and efficient, primarily because the communication paths have been shortened. This works in the spiritual realm too.

In removing the priests and others from the communication path, God has given us direct access to Him with all of the responsibilities and privileges that follow. Imagine if in our human love experiences that we could only talk to our sweetie indirectly—through three or four other persons. The relationship would not be near as close as it could be with direct communications. "Sweet nothings" would become nonexistent. It is the same with God. We become more formal and detached when we allow or rely upon additional participants. God removed the traditional additions to enable and encourage direct, intimate and personal communication with Him. Taking Him up on his offer is intimidating at first, but it is to our benefit to take the risk.

> *Gen. 1:2 – Now the earth was formless and empty, darkness was over the surface of the deep, and the Spirit of God was hovering over the waters. (NIV)*
>
> *1 Samuel 16:13 – Then Samuel took the horn of oil, and anointed him in the midst of his brethren: and the Spirit of the LORD came upon David from that day forward. So Samuel rose up, and went to Ramah.*
>
> *1 Samuel 10:10 – When they came there to the hill, there was a group of prophets to meet him; then the Spirit of God came upon him, and he prophesied among them. (NKJV)*
>
> *Mark 1:10-11 – And immediately, coming up from the water, He saw the heavens parting and the Spirit descending upon Him like a dove. Then a voice came from heaven, "You are My beloved Son, in whom I am well pleased." (NKJV)*
>
> *Romans 8:26-27 – Likewise the Spirit also helps in our weaknesses. For we do not know what we should pray for as*

we ought, but the Spirit Himself makes intercession for us with groanings which cannot be uttered. Now He who searches the hearts knows what the mind of the Spirit is, because He makes intercession for the saints according to the will of God. (NJKV)

2 Cor. 5:5 – Now it is God who has made us for this very purpose and has given us the Spirit as a deposit, guaranteeing what is to come. (NIV)

John 16:13-14 – However, when He, the Spirit of truth, has come, He will guide you into all truth; for He will not speak on His own authority, but whatever He hears He will speak; and He will tell you things to come. He will glorify Me, for He will take of what is Mine and declare it to you. (NKJV)

Acts 2:38-39 – Peter replied, "Repent and be baptized, every one of you, in the name of Jesus Christ for the forgiveness of your sins. And you will receive the gift of the Holy Spirit.

John 20:21-22 – So Jesus said to them again, "Peace to you! As the Father has sent Me, I also send you." And when He had said this, He breathed on them, and said to them, "Receive the Holy Spirit." (NKJV)

1 John 4:1-3 – Dear friends, do not believe every spirit, but test the spirits to see whether they are from God, because many false prophets have gone out into the world. This is how you can recognize the Spirit of God: Every spirit that acknowledges that Jesus Christ has come in the flesh is from God, but every spirit that does not acknowledge Jesus is not from God. This is the spirit of the antichrist, which you have heard is coming and even now is already in the world. (NIV)

1 Cor. 6:19-20 – Do you not know that your body is a

temple of the Holy Spirit, who is in you, whom you have received from God? You are not your own; you were bought at a price. Therefore honor God with your body. (NIV)

John 16:7-8 – But I tell you the truth: It is for your good that I am going away. Unless I go away, the Counselor will not come to you; but if I go, I will send him to you. When he comes, he will convict the world of guilt in regard to sin and righteousness and judgment. (NIV)

1 Cor. 12:4-12 – There are different kinds of gifts, but the same Spirit. There are different kinds of service, but the same Lord. There are different kinds of working, but the same God works all of them in all men. Now to each one the manifestation of the Spirit is given for the common good. To one there is given through the Spirit the message of wisdom, to another the message of knowledge by means of the same Spirit, to another faith by the same Spirit, to another gifts of healing by that one Spirit, to another miraculous powers, to another prophecy, to another distinguishing between spirits, to another speaking in different kinds of tongues, and to still another the interpretation of tongues. All these are the work of one and the same Spirit, and he gives them to each one, just as he determines. The body is a unit, though it is made up of many parts; and though all its parts are many, they form one body. So it is with Christ. (NIV)

[1] Edward K. Rowell, *1001 Quotes, Illustrations & Humorous Stories* for preachers, teachers and writers. (Grand Rapids MI: Baker Books, 2005), p.89.
[2] Derek Prince, *Baptism in the Holy Spirit* (New Kensington, PA: Whitaker House, 1995), p. 54
3 Ibid. p.19.
4 Ibid. p.31.
5 Ibid. p.34.

Chapter 6

The Search

The kingdom of heaven is like treasure hidden in a field. When a man found it, he hid it again, and then in his joy went and sold all he had and bought that field. Again, the kingdom of heaven is like a merchant looking for fine pearls. When he found one of great value, he went away and sold everything he had and bought it (Matthew 13:44-46 NIV).

Jesus taught in a lesson, *Ask, and it shall be given you; seek, and ye shall find; knock, and it shall be opened unto you: For every one that asketh receiveth; and he that seeketh findeth; and to him that knocketh it shall be opened.* One could easily interpret this lesson to mean that if we ask for material things, God will give them to us. If we ponder other complementary lessons collectively, the Holy Spirit reveals that Jesus was talking about us seeking God, not things. When we make God our primary priority, we then get all the other stuff we need as He sees fit, *But seek ye first the kingdom of God, and his righteousness; and all these things shall be added unto you.* Additionally, when God gives us things, we get *more than we can ask or imagine!* Our finite minds cannot fully comprehend the benefits of belonging to God.

The wonderful characteristic about God is that although He chooses to be invisible, He wants to reveal Himself to us. He sent His Son Jesus Christ to show us the way back to Him. If we seek Him with earnestness, humility, persistence, and honesty, we will find Him just as He guarantees, *I love those who love me, and those who seek me find me....* However, we must realize that God is a spirit and that human logic or science is not going to validate His existence. The world says, "I'll believe it when I see it." The Bible tells us that *without faith it is impossible to please God.* Thus, we will see God when we believe in Him. This is the essence of faith in God.

Counting the Cost

The value of anything can be measured by the cost of acquisition. Precious metals and stones are expensive because of the extensive effort required to extract them from the ground. Likewise, God appears to be a not-so-easy catch. He requires simple faith to get to Him, which is a substantial effort for human beings. It costs us everything to get to God and He is worth the cost.

Having attended church most of my life, I thought I never really had to search for God. Many divorce attorneys will confirm that familiarity is never a substitute for intimacy. I was baptized as a child and lived my life with a knowledge and belief in God. One day, I realized that something was missing, and this triggered a yearning that materialized as a search for what it was that I did not have.

The cost of my search was intent and time. An additional cost was giving up the tradition of church and the accompanying experiences. Surprisingly, those around me paid a cost as well. As we abandon traditional thoughts and beliefs, an unintended casualty is friends and family who do not understand or agree with our new approach towards God. Some of us even relapse to our former level of passivity because we cannot handle the impact on those around us.

> *Matt. 7:7-8 – Ask, and it shall be given you; seek, and ye shall find; knock, and it shall be opened unto you: For every*

one that asketh receiveth; and he that seeketh findeth; and to him that knocketh it shall be opened.

Matt. 6:33 – But seek ye first the kingdom of God, and his righteousness; and all these things shall be added unto you.

Eph. 3:20-21 – Now to him who is able to do immeasurably more than all we ask or imagine, according to his power that is at work within us, to him be glory in the church and in Christ Jesus throughout all generations, for ever and ever! Amen. (NIV)

Proverbs 8:17 – I love those who love me, And those who seek me diligently will find me. (NKJV)

Jer. 29:13 – And you will seek Me and find Me, when you search for Me with all your heart. (NKJV)

Isaiah 55:6-7 – Seek the LORD while he may be found; call on him while he is near. Let the wicked forsake his way and the evil man his thoughts. Let him turn to the LORD, and he will have mercy on him, and to our God, for he will freely pardon.

Hebrews 11:1 – Now faith is being sure of what we hope for and certain of what we do not see. (NIV)

Hebrews 11:6 – And without faith it is impossible to please God, because anyone who comes to him must believe that he exists and that he rewards those who earnestly seek him. (NIV)

Chapter 7

The Key

A buddy of mine forgot to give his young son an allowance one month. The child raised the issue when it was allowance time again by reminding his dad that he "owed him the previous month's allowance." My buddy lovingly corrected his son by informing him that he did not "owe" him anything. In his words, "I provide you with clothes, food, shelter, etc. because I love you. Likewise, through my grace I provide you an allowance. You cannot earn it." God does the same for us in providing eternal salvation; we can do nothing to earn it.

Grace

The word grace simply means, "unmerited favor." This means that we cannot earn it and we do not deserve it; we only have it because God wants us to have it. *Faith without works is dead,* but we often substitute doing stuff for faith, which can lead to busyness. We all have worked with someone who does a lot of work and generates much energy but does not seem to get anything accomplished. We can make the same mistake to the point of neglecting a central premise of salvation that grace is given and not earned.

We cannot "work" our way into the Kingdom of heaven. Neither can we live a life "good" enough to qualify us for eternal life with God, *for all have sinned and fall short of the glory of God*. Some of us believe that there is a spiritual "report card," and if we get more good marks than negative ones, we go to heaven. There is no biblical justification for this theory. The Bible does however reference the Book of Life as well as another book that keeps record of our deeds, not for whether we get in to heaven or not, but for the level of rewards after entrance is granted…*and the books were opened: and another book was opened, which is the book of life: and the dead were judged out of those things which were written in the books, according to their works.*

So how do we gain access to grace, since we cannot earn it? Faith is the door through which we step to obtain the grace of God. We should not have faith in faith or even faith in ourselves, but faith in Jesus Christ as the Son of God. He is the payment for the penalty for our separation from God, giving us access to God's grace. This would be the single, critical entry in the Book of Life. If we could work our way into eternal life with God, then the life, death and resurrection of Jesus would all be a great waste of time and suffering.

Faith

Faith is belief in something without having the physical evidence to justify it, *being sure of what we hope for and certain of what we do not see*. Salvation without faith is impractical, for *without faith it is impossible to please him: for he that cometh to God must believe that he is, and that he is a rewarder of them that diligently seek him*. We must believe that God exists in order to receive salvation from Him. Our struggle is that we rely on our eyes and scientific methodology for validation. This is dangerous because our eyes can be deceived by optical illusions like a mirage of water on a hot day where everything is dry and parched. Similarly, science is a poor source of validation because it relies on a theory as a fact until proven otherwise. The world was once "known" to be flat based upon credible scientific observations of the day. This fact proved to be incorrect over time, when actually it was incorrect at its formation.

By faith we believe that God is real, that Jesus and the Holy Spirit are real, and that there is a dilemma, which justifies the need for salvation. This problem is sin or separation from God. If we do not believe there is a God or that we have a sin issue, naturally we will not acknowledge any separation from God, which negates the role of salvation.

Gift of Salvation

Salvation is the gift God most desires to give us because he is *not wanting anyone to perish*. Salvation is being redeemed or saved from the penalty of sin, which is death. While we will die physically, our spirits will live forever. The question is: Where will our spirits live? Without Jesus, our spirits are condemned to eternal separation from God. God's commitment to our salvation is so great that He sent His Son Jesus to earth in order to show us the way back to Him. Because of the life, death, and resurrection of Jesus Christ, the debt for our sin has been paid.

In the Garden of Eden, God's original plan was an abundant one—immortal life for man with Him. Hence, when Adam disobeyed God and was kicked out of the Garden, God had to do something to enable us to reconcile our separation (sin) from Him. Adam was kicked out of the Garden because God told him that he would die if he ate from the Tree of the Knowledge of Good and Evil. The spiritual separation from God and eventual physical death had to occur, lest God tell an untruth, which is impossible, *For God is not a man, that He should lie*.

We might ask why God would give us a choice if He does not want us to have the possibility of experiencing eternal separation from Him. It is because He made us in His image by giving us "free will." Free will refers to the ability to choose between right and wrong. Man is the only creature on the planet that possesses this ability. Sure, monkeys and dolphins display limited intelligence, but not enough to determine their own destiny.

What we mistakenly interpret as intelligence in animals is often conditioning. Animals appear to be making rational choices by reacting to either punishment or reward. In giving us the option of choosing Him, God also gave us the option of not choosing Him. God wants us to serve and worship Him by our choice; otherwise, we would be like any other animal operating by instinct and not made in the image of God.

Our very nature rebels against God as we seek to do things our "own way" or even become our own god. Even those of us who are basically nice cannot save ourselves from the nature that is within each of us. Thank God that the gift of eternal salvation comes through grace received by a personal faith in Jesus Christ.

James 2:26 – For as the body without the spirit is dead, so faith without works is dead also. (NKJV)

Romans 3:22-24 – This righteousness from God comes through faith in Jesus Christ to all who believe. There is no difference, for all have sinned and fall short of the glory of God, and are justified freely by his grace through the redemption that came by Christ Jesus. (NIV)

Rev. 20:12 – And I saw the dead, small and great, stand before God; and the books were opened: and another book was opened, which is the book of life: and the dead were judged out of those things which were written in the books, according to their works.

Hebrews 11:6 – And without faith it is impossible to please God, because anyone who comes to him must believe that he exists and that he rewards those who earnestly seek him. (NIV)

2 Peter 3:9 – The Lord is not slow in keeping his promise, as some understand slowness. He is patient with you, not wanting anyone to perish, but everyone to come to repentance. (NIV)

Genesis 2:16-17 – And the LORD God commanded the man, saying, Of every tree of the garden thou mayest freely eat: But of the tree of the knowledge of good and evil, thou shalt not eat of it: for in the day that thou eatest thereof thou shalt surely die.

Numbers 23:19 – God is not a man, that he should lie, nor a son of man, that he should change his mind. Does he speak and then not act? Does he promise and not fulfill? (NIV)

Gal. 2:21 – I do not set aside the grace of God, for if righteousness could be gained through the law, Christ died for nothing!"

Chapter 8

The Way

There is a story told of an old farmer who lived by himself in a cabin. Next to his cabin was a barn. One very cold wintry night, birds began to crash into the windows of his warm cabin, trying to escape the deadly cold. So the old man went outside and opened the barn door. It was warm inside the barn. He waved his arms and shouted at the birds to go into the barn, into safety. But they did not understand him.

It was then that the old man wished that he could become one of them. If he could become a bird, then he could lead the other birds into the barn, to avoid death. And at that moment the old farmer understood why Jesus had come. Though the old man could not become a bird, God could become a man. So he did. *For God so loved the world that he sent his one and only Son, that whoever believes in him shall not perish, but have eternal life* (John 3:16).[1]

Jesus lived a perfect or sinless life while on earth. Although fully human, He did not separate Himself from God the Father through disobedience, idolatry, pride, or any of the other common human sins. Before we go any further, let us be very clear about whom we are speaking when we refer to Jesus. We are specifically speaking of Jesus of Nazareth who was born of a virgin named Mary in a town called Bethlehem, a descendent of David, the greatest King of Israel. A carpenter before He began working in the ministry full-time, Jesus was crucified (executed on a cross), buried, and rose from the dead on the third day. He is part of the Holy Trinity or Godhead as God the Son, along with God the Father and God the Holy Spirit. Jesus was fully man during His tenure on the earth and is fully God.

Jesus' Sacrifice

Jesus was led by the Holy Spirit into the wilderness to be tempted by the devil. Satan's tactic both then and now is to twist the Word of God to our demise, contrary to God's original intent. Jesus successfully countered the enticing offerings of Satan by not arguing with him; rather, He used the Word of God accurately and appropriately to defeat His enemy.

It might appear that Jesus' final statements on the cross, *"My God, My God, why have You forsaken Me?"* mark evidence of His sin. This is not true. Jesus quoted King David of Israel who had expressed similar feelings during a very low point in his life. Jesus was fully man, thus He was not immune to the pain and emotion that any of us would experience from being condemned and tortured for something we did not do. While fully God, Jesus could not avail Himself to His deity and still fulfill His purpose as the sacrificial Lamb. We have no idea of the cost required to pay the price for the sins of mankind. Jesus knew the cost and paid it despite His human reactions to an awful experience.

The key point to remember here is not what Jesus said, but what He did. *"Father, if you are willing, take this cup from me; yet not my will, but yours be done."* Committed to following God's commands, Jesus willingly endured a painful, agonizing, and humiliating human execution. It is true however, that He did not want to endure spiritual separation from God the Father—something He had never experienced.

The blood sacrifice is the highest offering that God requires. In the Old Testament, God required that a blood sacrifice pay or "atone" for the sins committed by man. *In fact, the law requires that nearly everything be cleansed with blood, for without the shedding of blood there is no forgiveness*. Accordingly, men would kill an innocent animal—usually a lamb—and sprinkle its blood upon the altar.

Adam's blatant disregard for God's warning in the Garden of Eden (that eating from the Tree of the Knowledge of Good and Evil would result in death) required such an atonement. This bold act of disobedience severed the fellowship or communion between God and man, a condition that we still deal with today. *For the wages of sin is death; but the gift of God is eternal life through Jesus Christ our Lord*. The penalty for this sin had to be paid if mankind was going to be reconciled back to God.

God has so much integrity that He cannot break His own rules regarding the required atonement for sin. He could not just let Adam's infraction occur without punishment and still be God. In the New Testament, God sent Jesus Christ—the only perfect, sinless sacrifice—to be the blood atonement or *the Lamb of God, who takes away the sin of the world*, so that we would not be separated from God for all eternity. This atonement must be applied or activated by faith in Jesus Christ as Lord and Savior.

This personal blood atonement is the major distinction between Christianity and other religions. Other religions worship persons claiming to be God, but who were, in fact, imperfect and fallible. Moreover, none personally offered themselves to be our blood atonement. Jesus—God the Son—paid our sin debt by giving His life. If Jesus had sinned, He could not atone for our sins, for He would not be an acceptable sacrifice. Christianity would then be another philosophy or concept and not a relationship with the living God.

According to scripture, Mary Magdalene and another Mary were the first people to see Jesus at the tomb. Another sighting of

Jesus was by the disciples in the upper room behind a locked door. Jesus entered the room without unlocking the door. This is not so strange given that Jesus walked on water before His death and performed other supernatural feats over nature! A week later in the upper room, Jesus instructed "doubting" Thomas to put his finger on the nail marks in His hands and in His side, thereby revealing that Jesus obviously had flesh that could be touched.

Jesus appeared in various places in and around Jerusalem for 40 days after His resurrection. The writer Paul says that Jesus appeared to more than 500 of the brothers. This implies the women and children who saw Jesus were not counted, and the total number should actually be higher. Think about it. How could 500 people—especially those like the early Christians who suffered extreme persecution—be convinced and coordinated to tell the same lie?

The Disciples Changed

Christianity, although new, was still a viable threat to the Roman government and the Jewish religious power structure. Killing Jesus did not solve the problem; it only made it worse. After the crucifixion, the disciples, as well as other followers of Jesus, became dejected, scorned, and scattered in large part because they had initially thought Jesus was going to depose the Roman Empire to become an earthly king. Although the threats and pressures against Christians by the Roman government did not dissipate, the disciples had changed dramatically.

Clearly something happened during the period between the crucifixion and when Peter preached to 3,000 people who became believers. The disciples saw Jesus, spoke with Him, and touched Him after the resurrection. They knew without a doubt that Jesus was not dead. Additionally, they had received the Holy Spirit as He had promised. Thus, in Acts 2:14, these same broken and scattered disciples were now bold in their proclamation of the resurrection of Jesus even with the threat of martyrdom that for most of them became a personal reality.

Only One Path

Contrary to popular opinions, there is only ONE way, avenue, or path to God Almighty and that is through Jesus Christ. Western philosophies promote tolerance of other opinions, but God is sovereign and His kingdom is not a democracy. God is not seeking our opinions on His existence nor His directives. In addition, belief in Jesus Christ is mutually exclusive; i.e., we cannot believe in Jesus Christ and still believe in other paths to God (Buddhism, Transcendental Meditation, New Age and Eastern Religions, Islam, Mormonism, etc.). These other religions may acknowledge Jesus as a great teacher and man—or even a prophet—but they nevertheless deny that Jesus is God.

All major religions are NOT serving the same God by a different name. Jesus is so bold in His pronouncement of who He is that He eliminates all other options. *Jesus saith unto him, I am the way, the truth, and the life: no man cometh unto the Father, but by me*. Jesus did not merely show the way to God, He is the only way to God. Jesus is the Son of God as part of the Holy Trinity.

Unlike the farmer at the start of this chapter, who could not personally demonstrate to the birds how to make it to safety in the barn, God came to earth as a man to provide us the way back to Him. He had to do it because otherwise we would never make it, and He wants us to make it much more than the farmer wanted the birds to be safe. Furthermore, God does not desire that we only make it into the barn. He is in the barn and desires that we hang out with Him there.

Matt. 4:1-4 – Then Jesus was led up by the Spirit into the wilderness to be tempted by the devil. And when He had fasted forty days and forty nights, afterward He was hungry. Now when the tempter came to Him, he said, "If You are the Son of God, command that these stones become bread." 4But He answered and said, "It is written, "Man shall not live by bread alone, but by every word that proceeds from the mouth of God."' (NKJV)

Psalm 22:1 – My God, My God, why have You forsaken Me? Why are You so far from helping Me, And from the words of My groaning? (NKJV)

Luke 22:42 – "Father, if you are willing, take this cup from me; yet not my will, but yours be done." (NIV)

Romans 3:25-26 – God presented him as a sacrifice of atonement, through faith in his blood. He did this to demonstrate his justice, because in his forbearance he had left the sins committed beforehand unpunished– he did it to demonstrate his justice at the present time, so as to be just and the one who justifies those who have faith in Jesus. (NIV)

Lev.17:11 – For the life of the flesh is in the blood: and I have given it to you upon the altar to make an atonement for your souls: for it is the blood that maketh an atonement for the soul.

1 John 4:9-10 – This is how God showed his love among us: He sent his one and only Son into the world that we might live through him. This is love: not that we loved God, but that he loved us and sent his Son as an atoning sacrifice for our sins. (NIV)

Heb. 9:22-26 – In fact, the law requires that nearly everything be cleansed with blood, and without the shedding of blood there is no forgiveness. (NIV)

Romans 6:23 – For the wages of sin is death; but the gift of God is eternal life through Jesus Christ our Lord. (KJV)

John 1:29 – The next day John seeth Jesus coming unto him, and saith, Behold the Lamb of God, which taketh away the sin of the world.

Acts 2:41 – Then they that gladly received his word were baptized: and the same day there were added unto them about three thousand souls.

John 14:6 – Jesus saith unto him, I am the way, the truth, and the life: no man cometh unto the Father, but by me.

Matt. 16:15-16 – He said to them, "But who do you say that I am?" Simon Peter answered and said, "You are the Christ, the Son of the living God." (NKJV)

Matt. 1:18-21 – Now the birth of Jesus Christ was as follows: After His mother Mary was betrothed to Joseph, before they came together, she was found with child of the Holy Spirit. Then Joseph her husband, being a just man, and not wanting to make her a public example, was minded to put her away secretly. But while he thought about these things, behold, an angel of the Lord appeared to him in a dream, saying, "Joseph, son of David, do not be afraid to take to you Mary your wife, for that which is conceived in her is of the Holy Spirit. And she will bring forth a Son, and you shall call His name JESUS, for He will save His people from their sins." (NKJV)

Col. 2:8-10 – See to it that no one takes you captive through hollow and deceptive philosophy, which depends on human tradition and the basic principles of this world rather than on Christ. For in Christ all the fullness of the Deity lives in bodily form, and you have been given fullness in Christ, who is the head over every power and authority. (NIV)

1 Cor. 15:3-7 – For what I received I passed on to you as of first importance: that Christ died for our sins according to the Scriptures, that he was buried, that he was raised on the third day according to the Scriptures, and that he appeared to Peter, and then to the Twelve. After that, he appeared to more than five hundred of the brothers at the same time, most of whom are still living, though some have fallen asleep. (NIV)

[1] Author unknown.

Chapter 9

The Roadmap

Sarah accepted a new job in Seattle, Washington. The hiring company agreed to pay her moving expenses from Virginia. Sarah decided to rent a truck and move herself, consequently pocketing the savings, which is acceptable according to the corporate guidelines. Her brother, Mark, always wanted to drive across county, so he agreed to help drive.

As Sarah meticulously packed her possessions, her brother stopped by the house.

"Did you get the road atlas and map out the trip?" she inquired.

"No, I've got it all up here," replied Mark as he pointed to his temple.

"You've got nothing," she countered. "How do you expect us to get to Seattle? I don't have time for one of your hair-brained adventures. We have a week to get there and set up the house I'm renting," she continued.

"Aw, relax, Sis," Mark responded, "it will be ok."

"Ok? Do you remember the time you wanted to drive me to Boston when I first moved back home? We ended up in Pittsburgh," she recalled. They both laughed, releasing the building tension.

"I love you, Brother, but without a map, I'm not going around the corner with you," Sarah insisted.

"Ok Sis, I'll get the road atlas and trace the journey with a highlighter. I might even calculate the breaks for gas and food," he concluded. They hugged and laughed again, then Sarah returned to packing.

Jesus Is the Way

Knowing there is a God and getting to Him are two totally different realities. It is obvious that California exists, yet we cannot get there from Ohio by continuing to drive east, regardless of our intent. Likewise, we cannot reach God and live with Him eternally by being good, *for all have sinned and fallen short of the glory of God*. The attempt displays initiative, but the desired outcome will never be achieved this way.

There is a personal reality that each of us must address: Every human being has the spiritual predisposition to separate from God (commit sin). The cost or penalty for our separation from God is death. God made provision for the penalty of sin a long time ago through Jesus. If we believe Jesus paid our debt and that He was raised from the dead, we have resolved the situation.

Jesus Christ is the way, path and door to get to God. Achieving eternal life with God without Jesus is impossible. If you have reached this page in the book and recognize that you do not know Jesus Christ as Lord and Savior in your life, and you desire to rectify this condition, do the following:

1. Confess (agree with God) that you have a sinful nature and have fallen short of God's Glory (that you can never be "good" enough for God).

2. Believe that Jesus Christ is Lord of all and that God raised Him from the dead.

3. Confess (out loud to other Christians) "Jesus is Lord" and " I accept Jesus Christ as my personal Lord and Savior."

4. Be baptized by water as soon as possible as a public statement that you have accepted Jesus as your Lord and Savior.

Here is an example of a prayer you can personalize and use:

Father God Almighty, I agree and confess that I have a sin-filled nature and I can never be good enough by myself for you. I believe that Jesus Christ is the Son of God, was crucified and died, and that you raised Him from the dead. I receive Jesus Christ as Lord and Savior of my life. I thank you for the gift of salvation and I commit my life to you. In the name of Jesus I pray, amen.

If the world could be saved through human kindness or clear thinking, Jesus either would have formed a sensitivity group and urged us to share our feelings or would have founded a school and asked us to have discussions,. But knowing the ways of God, the way of the world, and the persistence of human sin, he took up the cross, called disciples, gathered the church and bade us to follow him down a different path of freedom.[1]

Romans 3:22-24 – This righteousness from God comes through faith in Jesus Christ to all who believe. There is no difference, for all have sinned and fall short of the glory of God, and are justified freely by his grace through the redemption that came by Christ Jesus. (NIV)

Romans 6:23 – For the wages of sin is death; but the gift of God is eternal life through Jesus Christ our Lord.

Romans 5:8 – But God demonstrates his own love for us in this: While we were still sinners, Christ died for us. (NIV)

Romans 10:8-10,13 – But what does it say? "The word is

near you; it is in your mouth and in your heart," that is, the word of faith we are proclaiming: That if you confess with your mouth, "Jesus is Lord," and believe in your heart that God raised him from the dead, you will be saved. For it is with your heart that you believe and are justified, and it is with your mouth that you confess and are saved. for, Everyone who calls on the name of the Lord will be saved. (NIV)

Mark 16:16 – Whoever believes and is baptized will be saved, but whoever does not believe will be condemned. (NIV)

John 3:3-8 – In reply Jesus declared, "I tell you the truth, no one can see the kingdom of God unless he is born again." "How can a man be born when he is old?" Nicodemus asked. "Surely he cannot enter a second time into his mother's womb to be born!" Jesus answered, "I tell you the truth, no one can enter the kingdom of God unless he is born of water and the Spirit. Flesh gives birth to flesh, but the Spirit gives birth to spirit. You should not be surprised at my saying, 'You must be born again.' The wind blows wherever it pleases. You hear its sound, but you cannot tell where it comes from or where it is going. So it is with everyone born of the Spirit."(NIV)

[1] Edward K.Rowell, *1001 Quotes, Illustrations & Humorous Stories* for preachers, teachers and writers. (Grand Rapids MI: Baker Books, 2005), p.150.

Chapter 10

The Conversation

This, then, is how you should pray: "Our Father in heaven, hallowed be your name, your kingdom come, your will be done on earth as it is in heaven. Give us today our daily bread. Forgive us our debts, as we also have forgiven our debtors. And lead us not into temptation, but deliver us from the evil one" (Matt. 6:9-13).

Jesus presumed that His followers would pray and fast regularly after He returned to heaven because He used the term "when" instead of "if" when referencing prayer and fasting. He took time to specifically teach the discipline of prayer to His disciples. "Prayer is not one-sided communication with a distant God. Prayer is a conversation between you and God, a relationship between you and your Creator."[1] Prayer is a significant tool for Christians that is often misunderstood and obviously underutilized given the condition of the world.

A weekly prayer at the church service is not sufficient; neither is reciting a prayer with which we do not understand nor agree. Many of us have delegated our prayer responsibilities to certain people in positions of authority. Whether they are seminary graduates, ordained ministers, or elders in the church, having someone else pray for us all the time is not God's will. Would you permit someone else to speak with your spouse on your behalf 99% of the time? It is in our best interest to pray to God daily so that we can nurture our individual relationship with Him.

Fasting is another aspect of our spiritual life. When combined with prayer, it gives greater clarity for a couple of reasons. First, the body is not distracted by the digestive function. The acquisition, preparation, consumption, and digestion of food requires significant time, effort, energy, and thought. (This explains how the world approaches fasting.) Second, fasting compels us believers to deny ourselves and place our body under subjection of our spirit. This causes a shift in our focus from a material need, such as eating, towards a spiritual need, such as God and His agenda.

Combining fasting with prayer can yield powerful results. "If every Christian fasted, the results would shake our society like a windstorm bending a sapling. Christians would demonstrate that they live differently, that their faith is imperative, that the Almighty works in their daily lives."[2]

Isaiah 58 talks about fasting the way God intends. For example, we cannot cheat and take advantage of people while fasting and still claim the spiritual benefits of fasting. God is looking for people who will view injustice as He does but will also come to Him in prayer about it rather than complain or do nothing about the situation.

Some Reasons Why Christians Do Not Pray:

Ignorance— We do not know how because we never have been taught properly.

Laziness— Prayer is work. Discipline is necessary.

Fear— What if God says something back to me?

Pride— We will not humble ourselves to approach God.

Sin— God will not tolerate sin in His presence without confession and turning away from the sin.

Relationship experts often cite lack of communication as the root cause of relationship breakdowns. This potential disconnect can also occur between God and us. If we do not communicate with Him, our relationship never grows and eventually withers away. It is not like we communicate with a concept or idea; we communicate with living things. God is real, living, and conscious and awaiting us to enter into personal communication with Him.

Making Prayer Productive

Here are some suggestions to make your prayer time more productive. First, find out what the Bible has to say about prayer. Look up every scripture on prayer you can find, meditate on them, and ask God for deeper clarification. Second, go to a Christian bookstore and find a book on prayer that gives allegiance to Jesus Christ as Lord and Savior so that you may better understand prayer. Third, check with your church or your Christian friends' churches for a class on prayer, register and take the class. Finally, go talk with the intercessors at your local church. They give special attention to prayer and probably understand it a little better than most people.

Matt. 6:6 – But when you pray, go into your room, close the door and pray to your Father, who is unseen. Then your Father, who sees what is done in secret, will reward you.

Mark 1:35 – Very early in the morning, while it was still dark, Jesus got up, left the house and went off to a solitary place, where he prayed.

James 5:14-16 – Is any sick among you? let him call for the elders of the church; and let them pray over him, anointing him with oil in the name of the Lord: And the prayer of faith shall save the sick, and the Lord shall raise him up; and if he have committed sins, they shall be forgiven him. Confess your faults one to another, and pray one for another, that ye may be healed. The effectual fervent prayer of a righteous man availeth much.

James 4:1-3 – What causes fights and quarrels among you? Don't they come from your desires that battle within you? You want something but don't get it. You kill and covet, but you cannot have what you want. You quarrel and fight. You do not have, because you do not ask God. When you ask, you do not receive, because you ask with wrong motives, that you may spend what you get on your pleasures.

Eph. 6:18 – And pray in the Spirit on all occasions with all kinds of prayers and requests. With this in mind, be alert and always keep on praying for all the saints.

1 John 5:14-15 – And this is the confidence that we have in him, that, if we ask any thing according to his will, he heareth us: And if we know that he hear us, whatsoever we ask, we know that we have the petitions that we desired of him.

John 15:7 – If ye abide in me, and my words abide in you, ye shall ask what ye will, and it shall be done unto you.

Mark 11:24 – Therefore I tell you, whatever you ask for in prayer, believe that you have received it, and it will be yours.

Matt. 18:19-20 – Again I say to you that if two of you agree on earth concerning anything that they ask, it will be done for them by My Father in heaven. For where two or three are gathered together in My name, I am there in the midst of them." (NKJV)

Matt. 6:16 – When you fast, do not look somber as the hypocrites do, for they disfigure their faces to show men they are fasting. I tell you the truth, they have received their reward in full.

[1]T.W. Hunt and Claude V. King, *In God's Presence* (Nashville, TN: Lifeway Press), p. 12

[2]Elmer L. Towns, *Fasting for Spiritual Breakthrough* (Venture, CA: Regal Books), p.15

Chapter 11

The Abundance

My brother and his new wife were escorted to their bridal suite in an elegant hotel in the wee hours of the morning. They were tired from the many hours at their wedding reception and from mingling with their guests. They took a look around their room, taking in the sofa, chairs and table. But where was the bed? This was the bridal suite?

Then they discovered the sofa was a hide-a-bed, complete with lumpy mattress and springs sagging to the floor. My brother and his new wife spent a fitful night on the hide-a-bed, waking up with sore backs.

The next morning, the new husband went to the hotel desk and gave the management a tongue-lashing for giving them such a terrible room for the bridal suite.

"Did you open the door in the room?" was the response. When my brother went back up to the room, he opened a door they had thought was the closet. There, complete with fruit baskets and chocolates, was a beautiful bedroom."[1]

Too many believers are sleeping on the spiritual "hide-a-bed" like the couple in the above story, either not knowing there is a "bridal suite" or how to get to it. Jesus said, *"I have come that they may have life, and that they may have it more abundantly."*

Intangibles

Abundance is often mistaken to imply only financial wealth. On the contrary, God is interested in every aspect of a believer's life. Some of the areas where abundance should be evident include but are not limited to the intangibles of *love, joy, peace, patience, kindness, goodness, faithfulness, gentleness and self-control*. These are also the fruit of the Holy Spirit or the characteristics of God. Every thoughtful father wants his offspring to take on his good character traits, and so does God the Father. Note that these characteristics cannot be purchased, nor can a monetary value be assigned to them.

Physical Health

Physical health is another area of abundant living that believers can attain more than is prevalent today. While a controversial topic within the church, it is interesting to observe that Jesus did not heal everyone, yet He healed everyone with whom He came into contact. Every believer may or may not be healed while on this earth, but one could argue that a much greater percentage of believers should be able to receive physical, emotional and mental healing than currently do. The Gospel writer John mentioned that he desired that readers of his writings would *prosper and be in good health*. As one of Jesus' disciples, John had walked with Jesus for three years and surely understood that Jesus was very interested in healing during His ministry years.

Finances

Regarding our finances, *the blessing of the Lord brings wealth, and He adds no trouble to it*. This implies that there are no catches or hidden agendas with God. He is very clear about the requirement that He is number one, the top dog. God would not promise blessings without sorrow if He did not intend to keep His word. His promise is consistent with His character, not our self-centered desires. God has an assignment for each of us, and He will provide all the resources for us to be successful. Are we working on His assignments or have we commissioned our own assignment?

The Bible also cautions against laziness and not working: *If a man will not work, he shall not eat*. It sounds harsh, but the Bible encourages hard work, diligence and discipline. Paul stressed hard work to the degree that he continued to make tents (one of his many skills) even while he was busy starting churches, so as not to be a burden to new churches that could not afford to pay him.

Available Resources

There are several resources available to believers for attaining the abundant life that Jesus promised. **One resource is Jesus Christ,** the Son of God who calls us joint heirs with Him. He commits to share His heavenly inheritance with believers. Anything that Jesus inherits probably is worth receiving. Jesus also prays on the behalf of believers to the Father. *He is at the right hand of God and is also interceding for us*. Talk about a prayer partner!

Our second resource is the Holy Spirit. Imagine a personal life coach or counselor for every believer. Unlike so-called human advisors, the Holy Spirit has perfect knowledge in every situation and wants the best for His protègés. *And He who searches our hearts knows the mind of the Spirit because the Spirit intercedes for the saints in accordance with God's will*. Additionally, the Holy Spirit also intercedes to the Father for believers and reveals what the Father gives Him for believers to know. No selfish motives, attitudes, or jealousies reside with this counselor. Many successful people can attribute their success to a human mentor who had experienced many potential obstacles and advised them how to overcome them. What could we accomplish with a perfect mentor who has no human imperfections?

A third resource that is often neglected, the Bible is a very powerful tool covered elsewhere in this book. God is faithful and responsible for what He said. Not knowing what He said about our respective situation is not only silly, but potentially dangerous.

God has THE plan (not a plan) for every believer's life, *"For I know the plans I have for you," declares the LORD, "plans to prosper you and not to harm you, plans to give you hope and a future."* The plan was made before we developed in our mother's womb. Following God's plan by believing Him, doing the work, and reaping the perks could be the definition of success and prosperity—doing what God purposed us to do and benefiting from being obedient. Our challenge is to use God's method of operation, not our own. Neither material abundance nor any person can ever take the place of God because it would be idolatry. God will never tolerate idolatry. Contemplate spiritual idolatry as physical adultery, and we begin to understand God's perspective on infidelity.

The apostle Paul appears to sum up the abundant life question, *And my God shall supply all your need according to His riches in glory by Christ Jesus*. The disciple Matthew adds this caveat, *But seek ye first the kingdom of God, and his righteousness; and all these things shall be added unto you*. We live in a stuff-obsessed culture, so breaking clear of this mindset is very challenging but not impossible to achieve. NEED is the key word, not WANT. There is a world of difference between the two terms.

Lack of an abundant life is what caused me to revisit my status with God. I believed in Jesus as the risen Son of God and had willingly been baptized as a child, yet something was amiss. I truly believed I would go to heaven after dying (not because I deserved it), but I was increasingly uncomfortable with a "suffer now and get rewarded later" approach to salvation sometimes presented by the Church. This struck me as a prescription for religious-sanctioned mediocrity.

I had fasted a few months prior to this new revelation, erroneously seeking something from God as if my little denial of food would move heaven to respond to my selfish request. I clearly heard the Spirit of God (in my spirit, not my ears) say to me, "You are trying to get something from Me; get Me." I was caught in the act or "cold busted" as we used to say as kids. I felt so insignificant, yet God now had my attention for a setup that we will address shortly.

Every one of us human beings is required to consciously decide if we want to be a believer and follower of Jesus Christ. We then have the opportunity to live the life abundantly that Jesus promises by graciously going into the bridal suite, or we can sleep on the couch in the spiritual foyer as did the couple in the beginning of this chapter.

John 10:10 – The thief cometh not, but for to steal, and to kill, and to destroy: I am come that they might have life, and that they might have it more abundantly.(NIV)

Gal. 5:22-23 – But the fruit of the Spirit is love, joy, peace, longsuffering, kindness, goodness, faithfulness, gentleness, self-control. Against such there is no law. (NKJV)

3 John 1:2 – Beloved, I pray that you may prosper in all things and be in health, just as your soul prospers. (NKJV)

Prov. 10:22 – The blessing of the LORD brings wealth, and he adds no trouble to it. (NIV)

2 Thess. 3:10 – For even when we were with you, we gave you this rule: "If a man will not work, he shall not eat." (NIV)

Heb. 9:15 – For this reason Christ is the mediator of a new covenant, that those who are called may receive the promised eternal inheritance—now that he has died as a ransom to set them free from the sins committed under the first covenant. (NIV)

Romans 8:34 – Who is he that condemns? Christ Jesus, who died—more than that, who was raised to life—is at the right hand of God and is also interceding for us. (NIV)

Romans 8:27 – And he who searches our hearts knows the mind of the Spirit, because the Spirit intercedes for the saints in accordance with God's will. (NIV)

Jer. 1:4-5 – "Before I formed you in the womb I knew you, before you were born I set you apart; I appointed you as a prophet to the nations." (NIV)

Jer. 29:11-12 – "For I know the plans I have for you," declares the LORD, "plans to prosper you and not to harm you, plans to give you hope and a future. (NIV)

Phil. 4:19 – And my God shall supply all your need according to His riches in glory by Christ Jesus. (NKJV)

Matt. 6:33 – But seek ye first the kingdom of God, and his righteousness; and all these things shall be added unto you.

Isaiah 55:10-11 – For as the rain cometh down, and the snow from heaven, and returneth not thither, but watereth the earth, and maketh it bring forth and bud, that it may give seed to the sower, and bread to the eater: So shall my word be that goeth forth out of my mouth: it shall not return unto me void, but it shall accomplish that which I please, and it shall prosper in the thing whereto I sent it.

[1] Edward K.Rowell , *1001 Quotes, Illustrations & Humorous Stories* for preachers, teachers and writers. (Grand Rapids MI: Baker Books, 2005), p.469.

Chapter 12

The Victory

The Department of Transportation has set aside 200 million dollars for research and testing of an Automated Highway System. This system would purportedly relieve traffic woes with "super cruise control" in heavily congested areas.

Special magnets imbedded in the asphalt every four feet would transfer signals between vehicle and main computer system. Steering, acceleration, and braking would be controlled by sensors, computer navigation systems, and cameras along the side of the road. Control would be returned to drivers at their specified exit.

Researchers and government officials claim they have the technological capability to address any potential problem. The one challenge they have yet to address?

Says Mike Doble, Buick's technology manager, "The only thing we can't do yet is get people to comfortably trust the system. It's not a technology issue. Would you drive, closely spaced, at high speeds, through San Diego?"

Trust is always the question. *"Trust in the LORD with all your heart and lean not on your own understanding; in all your ways acknowledge him, and he will make your paths straight"* (Prov. 3:5-6).[1]

Submission is often perceived as a risk, due to a suspicion that the recipient of the submission will take advantage of the one submitting. Conversely, God is the best Person to whom we can submit. One can go through all of the steps to become a believer in Jesus Christ, yet still miss most of the benefit package. This would be akin to working and not receiving a full paycheck with the promise of a great pension upon retirement. Many Christians (including me) got the "Savior" part of Jesus' offer but neglected to sign up for the "Lord" part of the program to our own detriment.

Lordship

Lordship is a difficult concept for us living within democratic style governments. Our representative approach to government makes it challenging for us to fully comprehend kings, kingdoms and lordship. Submitting our very lives to Jesus may be uncomfortable and is clearly unusual. We prefer to remain in charge, the captain of our ship; yet we are called to *submit to God, resist the devil and he will flee....* It is, however, impossible to submit and remain in control. This is like driving with the brake engaged. We retain free will to choose or not choose God's direction, yet spiritual power is achieved through submission.

One of the paradoxical statements in the Bible says that God is strong in our weakness. This means that when we surrender our agenda and approach for our lives that God can then work His perfect plan through us, *"For I know the plans I have for you," declares the LORD, "plans to prosper you and not to harm you, plans to give you hope and a future. Then you will call upon me and come and pray to me, and I will listen to you."*

Every father wants the best for his children. Yet God is a different type of father in that He has the best to give and He is not limited by space, time or any other physical parameters. He knows everything, He is everywhere, and He has all power. Not trusting God could be our major stumbling block.

I mentioned previously about God getting my attention during an unsuccessful fast. He responded to my selfishly inspired fast by saying, "You are trying to get something from Me; get Me." I ended the fast remembering His words, but not sure what to do with them. Needless to say, I was humbled. A few months later I was reflecting upon my life and concluded that I did not like it. I recall thinking that none of my plans were coming to fruition outside of educational achievements. I was not pleased with my income, career or anything else. I should have been married with children by then, I thought. I summarized my life as incomplete in most areas.

Something was missing. I attended church regularly. I was studying and teaching the Bible. I knew about the promises of God for believers, but I was not living that reality. I felt powerless, yet I knew it should not be this way.

Trying It His Way

I had reached my lowest point when I perceived that I understood the degree of despair that could push a person to suicide, but I was too afraid of God to contemplate this solution. As a result, I shifted gears and had a brief conversation with God. It went something like this, "God, my way is not working. Let's try it your way." God honored this simple, yet powerfully humble prayer with a chain of events that is continuing to this day. I had never totally submitted my life, agenda, dreams, goals or thoughts to God. Somehow I missed this simple step in my life as a believer. Following this honest plea to the Father, I learned about the power of the Holy Spirit, whom I had studied and taught a Bible study about the previous year. I asked for the Holy Spirit and received Him as Jesus promises.

God's power now works in me to achieve His purpose for my life and others. I am not perfect, but I am eternally grateful that God saw fit to not only save me from death and destruction, but to use me in various ways. I am grateful that God was not satisfied to leave me in a passive, non-fruitful relationship with Him, but drew me closer to Him. Additionally, I am totally convinced that submission is a major stumbling block for believers because we do not understand it and everything in our western culture goes against it.

Trust is the issue. Do we trust God enough to surrender our self-determination and submit to Him even though our natural inclination is the exact opposite? Unless we do so, we will experience a constant void in our soul that cannot be resolved any other way.

> *James 4:7 – Submit yourselves, then, to God. Resist the devil, and he will flee from you.*
>
> *2 Cor. 12:9-11 – But he said to me, "My grace is sufficient for you, for my power is made perfect in weakness." Therefore I will boast all the more gladly about my weaknesses, so that Christ's power may rest on me. That is why, for Christ's sake, I delight in weaknesses, in insults, in hardships, in persecutions, in difficulties. For when I am weak, then I am strong. (NIV)*
>
> *Acts 1:8 – But you shall receive power when the Holy Spirit has come upon you; and you shall be witnesses to Me in Jerusalem, and in all Judea and Samaria, and to the end of the earth. (NKJV)*

[1] Edward K.Rowell, *1001 Quotes, Illustrations & Humorous Stories* for preachers, teachers and writers. (Grand Rapids MI: Baker Books, 2005), p.395.

Chapter 13

The Invitation

The key issue is relationship. The quality of our relationship with God is determined by our obedience through the power of the Holy Spirit. Religion cannot save us. God will not ask us our religion or denomination on Judgment Day. Neither will He ask us the name of our pastor, favorite charity, or church. The only character reference God will take on our behalf is from Jesus Christ. Do you know about Him or do you know Him? Does He know you?

Since God is a living being, we have to communicate with Him. God is not impersonal or detached. He loves us very much and is calling each of us to an intimate relationship with Himself. Following Jesus makes us one of His disciples.

Christian discipleship is developing a personal, lifelong, obedient relationship with Jesus Christ in which He transforms your character into Christlikeness; changes your values into Kingdom values; and involves you in His mission in the home, the church and the world.[1]

Additionally, we can be effective disciples of Jesus Christ, by following six disciplines of discipleship. They include: 1) Spend time with the Master; 2) Live in the Word; 3) Pray in faith; 4) Fellowship with believers; 5) Witness to the world; and 6) Minister to others.[2]

A relationship that has not improved in 5-20 years is not a vibrant relationship. A relationship with no communication going back and forth is dead. Our living Lord and Savior is crying out to us in His Word and by His Holy Spirit to move past the pomp and circumstance of religion to know Him personally. Salvation is personal and our relationship with God must also be personal. We must abandon our perception of who God is and receive God's revelation of who He is.

Suppose that you have a sweetie. Would you seek him or her out only three or four times per year? How about only when you need something? How fruitful would that relationship be for either party? How long would such a relationship last? On the contrary, we look to spend as much time as practically possible with him or her. There is no one more loving and faithful than God. His very nature is pure love, and He pursues us relentlessly. All we have to do is receive His love and then reciprocate it. The relationship will flourish and all will be well with our soul.

Ask God through Jesus to show you how to get the relationship He desires. Submit to His agenda through the leading of the Holy Spirit and hold onto your hat. It is going to be an exciting and worthwhile journey.

> *John 14:21 – Whoever has my commands and obeys them, he is the one who loves me. He who loves me will be loved by my Father, and I too will love him and show myself to him." (NIV)*

> *John 14:23-24 – Jesus replied, "If anyone loves me, he will obey my teaching. My Father will love him, and we will come to him and make our home with him. He who does not love me will not obey my teaching. These words you hear are not my own; they belong to the Father who sent me. (NIV)*

[1]Avery T. Willis, Jr., and Kay Moore, *The Disciple's Cross: Masterlife Book 1*, (Nashville, TN: Lifeway Press, 1996), p.5

[2] Ibid.

Epilogue

It's not about you. It's not about me. This book may have been a review for some of us. For others, it may have been a handy primer. Regardless, we all can do better in our relationship with God through Jesus Christ. Part of our responsibility is to share this relationship with others.

If you know someone who will benefit from the information presented in this book, please share it with them and then follow up to see if they have questions. This is where your personal testimony can make the difference. It is not about recruiting or selling Jesus, but about telling what God has done for you. The divine setup has already been established. All of heaven is cheering you on, so go forward in confidence!

God bless you.
Patrick

For discussion questions on this book,
see the website listed below.

Contact Patrick at

P. McElroy
P.O. Box 1569
Loganville, GA 30052

visit his website at
www.beyondbeliefbook.com
for speaking engagements.

Recommended Reading List

Experiencing the Holy Spirit, Andrew Murray (New Kensington, PA: Whitaker House, 1984)

Baptism in the Holy Spirit, Derek Prince (New Kensington, PA: Whitaker House,1995)

In God's Presence (workbook), T.W. Hunt and Claude V. King (Nashville, TN: Lifeway Press, 1994)

The Disciple's Cross: Masterlife Book 1, Avery T. Willis, Jr., and Kay Moore (Nashville, TN: Lifeway Press, 1996), p.5

Experiencing God (workbook), Henry T. Blackaby & Claude V. King (Nashville, TN: Lifeway Press, 1990)

Fasting for Spiritual Breakthrough, Elmer L. Towns (Venture, CA: Regal Books, 1996)

About the Author

Patrick D. McElroy was born and raised in Dayton, Ohio. He currently resides in Atlanta, Georgia. He was baptized at twelve years old and although a believer since then, he rarely experienced any consistent spiritual power until one summer when he recognized and acknowledged that his approach to life was not producing the abundant life that Jesus had promised. He resolved to rectify this situation. This book is but one manifestation of God's divine calling upon his life.